CURSIVE
HANDWRITING
WORKBOOK

Notebooks, Journals,
Sketchbooks and Workbooks
by Genius Minds

Learn, develop and improve your penmanship with this workbook.

This book is designed for those who would like to either learn cursive hand writing or to practice and improve their writing form.
Develop the correct shape and slope for a seamless consistent flow and a more beautiful, legible style.

The art of handwriting is a wonderful skill to have for general writing, letter writing and for writing cards, invitations and much more.

Features

- The cursive style used is the standard, traditional American Cursive.
- Examples are with arrows to show the direction the letters are formed.
- Use trace over guides for the alphabet and words. Then continue with the guide lines to write them on your own.

- Practice individual letters, upper and lower case.
- Practice the sentence 'The quick brown fox jumps over the lazy dog.' which contains all the letters of the alphabet.
- There are extra pages with guidelines to continue practicing letters, words or sentences of your choice.

It can be more difficult to write on the left hand pages, but guide line have been included on those pages for you to utilize if you wish to.
Even without these there is plenty of writing space to practice.

A *Aa* B *Bb* C *Cc* D *Dd* E *Ee*

F *Ff* G *Gg* H *Hh* I *Ii* J *Jj*

K *Kk* L *Ll* M *Mm* N *Nn*

O *Oo* P *Pp* Q *Qq* R *Rr* S *Ss*

T *Tt* U *Uu* V *Vv* W *Ww* X *Xx*

Y *Yy* Z *Zz*

a a

B b

C c

D d

E e

E E E E E E E E E E E E

E E E E E E E E E E E E

e e e e e e e e e e e e e e e

e e e e e e e e e e e e e e e

e e e e e e e e e e e e e e e

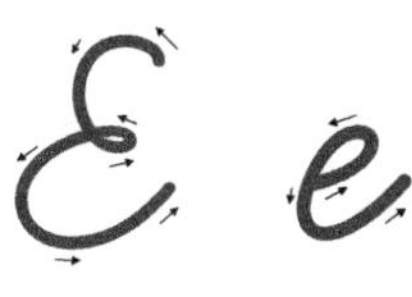

H h

K k

K K K K K K K K K K K

K K K K K K K K K K K

k k k k k k k k k k k k

k k k k k k k k k k k k

k k k k k k k k k k k k

$$\mathcal{L}\ \ell$$

M m

n, n

O o

O O O O O O O O O O O O

O O O O O O O O O O O O

o o o o o o o o o o o o o o o

o o o o o o o o o o o o o o o

o o o o o o o o o o o o o o o

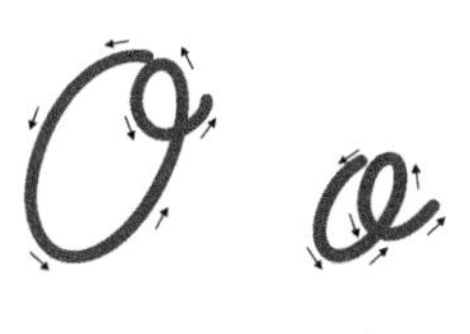

P p

R r

S s

S S S S S S S S S S S S

S S S S S S S S S S S S

s s s s s s s s s s s s s s s

s s s s s s s s s s s s s s s

s s s s s s s s s s s s s s s

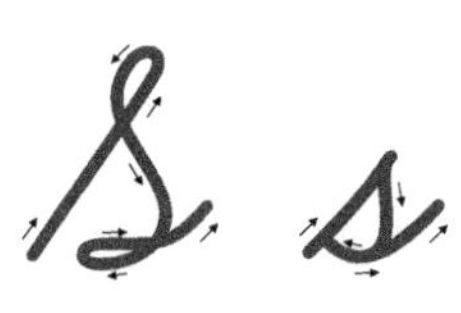

T t

И и

V u

$$W \, w$$

Y y

This sentence contains all the letter of the alphabet.

The quick brown fox jumps over the
lazy dog. The quick brown fox jumps
over the lazy dog. The quick brown
fox jumps over the lazy dog. The quick
brown fox jumps over the lazy dog.
The quick brown fox jumps over the
lazy dog. The quick brown fox jumps
over the lazy dog. The quick brown
fox jumps over the lazy dog.

Numbers

One one one one

Two two two two

Three three three

Four four four four

Five five five five

Six six six six

Seven seven seven seven

Eight eight eight eight

Nine nine nine nine

Ten ten ten ten

Days of the week.

Monday Monday

Tuesday Tuesday

Wednesday Wednesday

Thursday Thursday

Friday Friday

Saturday Saturday

Sunday Sunday

Months of the year.

January January

February February

March March

April April

May May

June June

July July

August August

September September

October October
November November
December December

My name is

I am from

I live in

I hope to

I also like to

I spend most of my days

Continue to write whatever you like.